Table Of Contents

AF409147

Introduction

I have been training dogs for over twenty five years. I do a lot of obedience and behavior training with most breeds of dogs. No matter what kind of dog you own, whether it is a puppy or an adult, a Yorkie, Chorkie, Maltese, German shorthair pointer, Australia Sheppard or an English setter, there are training methods that have been designed to help you to teach your dog the behaviors you want it to learn.

Unfortunately, there is not a one-size-fits-all, method. Puppies learn differently than adult dogs and hunting dogs need different training than dogs that are going to travel with you in your purse or travel bag.

This does not mean that you have to run out and buy a gazillion different books to find the right method to train your dog. It does mean that you need to understand what you want in a dog, what you expect it to learn and how much effort you are willing to put into your dog's training.

Some people expect their dogs to learn a lot, some only want the basics, and some have very explicit desires like a dog that will point a bird and not budge when that bird flushes. Some people want herding dogs, some want service dogs and some just want a companion that can keep the loneliness away.

Some of these behaviors are specialized and can't be covered in a general book about dog training, but a lot of it can be covered and I think you can learn quite a bit about dogs and dog training by reading this book. If you want to go beyond the basics that are taught in here, you will have a great foundation from which to start.

Understanding Your Dog

Let's start at the beginning. How do you pick the dog that will be your best friend for many years to come? Do you want an adult? Maybe you want a rescue or a shelter dog? How about a puppy? This is the first question that you need to answer.

Let's start from youngest to oldest and talk about what you might want to look for. Truth be told, it is easier to start training a small puppy than an older dog, but the training can be done at any age. One of the important keys to ease of training is intelligence. That is the main reason I always encourage a person to spend a considerable amount of time with your prospective new buddy; you want to bond easily with this dog/puppy and you want to be certain it is smart.

Extremely shy dogs and even most aggressive dogs are simply not very bright and they fear anything they do not understand and are not smart enough to rely on their owner to tell them if and when it is safe. Intelligent dogs can be a joy to train.

Key Takeaways:
- It is easier to train a puppy than an adult dog but training can be done at any age;
- The key to ease of training is: Intelligence.

Buying a Puppy: What Exactly is, "Pick of the Litter?"

If at all possible, when buying a puppy, try to meet the puppies and at least the mother of the pups before you pick out the one you want. If you cannot do that, think about what you want in a puppy and ask the owner/breeder/seller, to pick one that matches your description.

Some puppies and dogs are purchased from owners who live far away and will need to be shipped to their new owners, sight unseen. If the person asks you for a higher rate for "pick of the litter" or an extra fee for picking out a pup for you, find a different seller and a different litter of puppies. Never pay extra for "pick of the litter." What is the perfect dog for one person will not be the perfect dog for another. There really is no "best puppy."

The first question a breeder should ask a person who is looking for a dog or puppy, is, "What are you looking for in a dog?" He or she should then take the time to listen to that person's description.

Sometimes a breeder simply does not have what a person wants. That breeder should very honestly tell the person the truth and make suggestions where the person may want to look for the dog he or she would be happy with. A good breeder certainly does not want to sell a dog or puppy to a person and have them both be miserable; He or she would rather match the right dog/puppy with the right owner from the start.

Because I am a trainer, the pup I would choose to keep is most likely not the pup that you would choose to buy. You may be looking for a dog that will be quiet and sit with you by the fire and put its head on your knee while I want a dog that is a real go-getter and wants to be off and running at all times. Which of these is the pick of the litter?

None of us wants a sickly, shy or reclusive dog and if someone tries to sell you one because you did not fork over the extra money for pick of the litter, this person is actually being unethical, and may even be breaking the law or violating state and federal kennel regulations. "Pick of the litter" does not mean "the only healthy pup in the litter." If a puppy that is not healthy is sold to you, the breeder is responsible and should be contacted right away.

If you are not looking for a professionally bred dog or puppy, try to meet all of the puppies in a litter so you can pick out the one that stands out, to you, the most. Get down and play with the puppies; I guarantee that, before long, one will have captured your heart. Take your time and do not let the owner hurry you. You will be spending a long time with this little guy or gal and you want to take your time finding just the right puppy to meet your personal wishes.

Looking for a rescue or shelter dog? Do the same thing. Take some time and meet the dogs that are available and see how they each respond to you. I strongly recommend that you avoid dogs that appear to have been abused, neglected or are frightened of their own shadows. While it feels good to say that you have rescued an abused dog; the time, knowledge and patience required working with and bonding with one of these dogs is well beyond the scope of this book. Any dog brought into a new home from a shelter is one dog saved from either a lethal injection, the gas chamber, or a life spent in a very small cage. You are a hero for taking any dog from a shelter; it does not need to be the worst case there.

Once you have had a chance to play with and love-up the dog or pup that will be your best buddy, it is time to take your pal home and start its training.

Key Takeaways:
- Never pay extra for "pick of the litter";
- Try to meet all of the puppies in a litter;
- Get down and play with the puppies – before long, one will have captured your heart.

Introduction to Training

You may have heard that dog training methods have changed and you are right! Training methods have radically changed in the last ten years and the results have been phenomenal!

Changing from traditional methods (called Aversive-based training) to Positive, Reward-based training has actually resulted in fewer dogs being taken to shelters due to behavior problems! This is a fact. Dogs trained by these new methods stay trained longer, are far less prone to becoming violent and they are enjoyable to be around.

 This is not just some method developed by someone who thinks punishing a dog for misbehaving is bad; these are methods that have been studied scientifically. There has been new information about dog behavior just pouring out of laboratories and most of it has been very good news, indeed.

Bite Inhibition

Before I start in about some of these new methods and why they work, there is one new training development that I think is very important for everyone to teach their dog. This is called, bite inhibition, and it is something that can save you a tremendous headache and also save your dog from being put down because of aggressive behavior.

Basically, you do not just teach your dog not to bite, you teach your dog not to bite hard. Are you scratching your head? The first time I heard about this it took a few minutes for it to sink in. Suddenly, it was like a light went on in my head and it made a lot of sense.

Look at it this way; You can teach your dog that it is wrong to bite, then one day, someone walks by it with baseball cleats on and smash one of your dog's toes. That dog is suddenly in serious pain, is scared and confused and its basic instinct is to lash out and bite whoever is causing the pain. The next thing you know, that person is being rushed to the hospital to get twenty stitches in his leg and the local police officer is asking to see your dog's rabies certificate and talking about quarantining it.

Believe it or not, this could all have been avoided with bite inhibition training. Puppies actually begin this training when they are still with their mothers. If they bite her too hard when nursing, she gets up and walks away; if they bite a sibling too hard when playing, the sibling yips and stops playing. The puppy has had its first two lesions in bite inhibition. This is training you can keep up once you have the pup at home.

Let's face it, no one enjoys being nipped by a puppy; those teeth are really sharp. If you say "Owww" and stop playing with the puppy every time it bites you too hard or walk away from it or put the puppy in time out, the puppy learns not to bite hard. You do not scold it or slap it, which could make it bite all that much harder; you stop playing and leave the pup to be alone. Do this several times a day as a training activity.

When you do not want to do a training activity every time you are with your puppy, give it a toy to play with and chew on when it wants to playfully nip at you or your clothing and the puppy will learn what things it can play with. As the puppy learns to control the pressure of its bite, you can start requiring lighter and lighter pressure.

Occasionally reinforce this training for the life of your dog, and even if sudden problems occur or accidents happen, the dog will not bite as hard as it would have without the training. This is something all service dogs are taught in order to keep them from ever hurting their owners while helping them or hurting someone else if they are suddenly surprised. This training has saved many people from serious bites and many dogs and owners from serious consequences.

Key Takeaways:
- You do not just teach your dog not to bite, you teach your dog not to bite hard;
- Stop playing with the puppy every time it bites you too hard or walk away from it;
- Give it a toy to play with and chew on when it wants to playfully nip at you or your clothing;
- Occasionally reinforce this training for the life of your dog.

What do You Want Your Dog to Learn?

Depending on the breed and what you expect from your dog, you may want different behaviors from your dog than your next door neighbor.

If your neighbor has a German shorthair pointer that he takes hunting every weekend and you have a Yorkshire terrier that you like to put in a carrying case and take everywhere with you, you are both going to have different expectations from your dogs.

If your neighbor lives on a farm in an old rambling farmhouse and you live in an apartment on the tenth floor, you each may have some very different expectations when it comes to house-breaking.

Let's start with some basics and some explanations and then take it from there.

Training Puppies From Day #1

Traditional methods have always stated that you cannot start any serious training until you pup is six months old. This is because it takes that long for puppies to comprehend punishment and also, their little bodies are not powerful enough to withstand things like yanking hard on their collars to reprimand them.

Using the right techniques, you can have most of your training accomplished before your pup even hits the six month old mark. With reward-based training, your puppy is glad to do the things you want and it learns to quickly love and enjoy you without being afraid that you are going to yell or jerk it or slap it for no reason that it knows.

First, positive reinforcement does not mean that you allow your dog to run rampant, doing whatever it wants while you idly stand by without punishing it. It means you carefully control all of its behavior and reward it when it does things the way you want it to. Keep reading; it gets clearer.

Even before your new puppy comes home, get everything ready for it. This is very important. You want everything in place so the pup can learn where everything is and what is expected right from day #1.

Where is the puppy going to sleep? Remember, puppies do not sleep all night. They pretty much function on a three hour schedule, so you will have extra work for the first few weeks. If the puppy has an enclosed area ready with a special place to sleep, a place to move around and a place to relieve itself, you may just get away with sleeping through the night.

Of course, this special place really should be in your bedroom (sorry!), so that the pup knows you are close by. Some people simply have a plastic crate in the bedroom and get up every few hours to let the puppy out to pee or poop (more about that later).

So, your puppy needs a place of its own; a place to sleep, a place to play and a place where it can stay if you are going to leave it home alone at all. Many pet supply stores sell fenced enclosures for puppies that you can put into different shapes and sizes so your puppy can have a fenced in place somewhere in your house or apartment to call its own. This is actually very important because it will keep your puppy out of trouble when you cannot watch it and also have a place to put it when it gets a little too wound and needs a quiet place to calm down.

Little puppies go potty a lot. It will help if you have training pads in a special place and also in a small area in its enclosure where the puppy can go potty when in the enclosure.

Put the puppy on the pad, several times a day and give it whatever command you are going to use to tell it is time to potty. Have the spot close to where the puppy spends most of its time. You can actually move it further away, later.

At first, this is all simply timing. Pick up the puppy, set it on the pad and tell it to go potty. When it does this, praise it and tell it what a good little puppy it is. If the pad is close by, you will be surprised at how quickly the puppy learns to use it.

Each time the puppy uses the floor instead, do not correct it by yelling, just pick it up and set it on the pad to remind it of where it should have gone. As the puppy grows older and older, it will become more and more reliable at using the right spot.

If you live where the pup can use the outdoors to go potty, put the puppy outside frequently, and use the "potty" command. Because puppies go potty so often, it is good to have a place in the house, even if you will eventually want it to use the outdoors all the time when it gets older.

Moving the pad closer to the door and then moving the pad outside the door is a very easy method for changing the place for the pup to use.

Key Takeaways:
- With reward-based training you can start train your puppy from day #1;
- Positive reinforcement means you carefully control all of its behavior and reward it when it does things the way you want it to;
- Your puppy needs a place of its own; a place to sleep, a place to play and a place where it can stay if you are going to leave it home alone at all;
- Little puppies go potty a lot. It will help if you have training pads in a special place.

The Differences in Breed Behaviors

Dogs are frequently bred for different reasons and behaviors. A herding dog is bred to enhance its herding abilities. A hunting dog is bred for its great nose and desire to hunt, a racing dog is bred for speed and a companion dog is bred for being affectionate.

Selective breeding has done more in a few years than Darwin could have ever imagined. Breeders look at their dogs very thoroughly and carefully breed so that certain traits will be further enhanced. Unfortunately some breeders simply breed indiscriminately to get litter after litter, and this is the kind of breeding you want to avoid.

When I advised you to try to meet the parents of the puppy you are looking at, this selective breeding is what you are looking for. You want to be sure that the breeder is carefully breeding for certain characteristics, that it is simply not a "puppy mill" with less than ideal facilities and that the parents are smart and possess the personality you are looking for in a dog.

Remember, if the parents do not have the kind of personality you want in your dog, there is an excellent chance that neither will your puppy. If you already have an idea of the perfect puppy or dog in your head, it will help you to look at how the parents behave and then at the pups that are available.

This will help you to know if any of the puppies have those traits you want in your best buddy. If you do not see those traits in the parents or in any of the puppies, find someone else who is offering pups for sale.

Stand-offish and shy puppies are problems in the making because they may be less intelligent than you would like. The boldest fire-breather in the litter may be the ideal dog for a breeder, but this puppy could end up being someone's problem child that expects everyone to worship the ground it walks on. Meanwhile, the puppy that just wants to curl up in your lap and be close to you could be the one that is destined to be your best friend for years to come.

Small and toy dogs are bred specifically to be companion dogs and these little bundles of love will want to be with you, 24 hours a day, 7 days a week. If you plan to keep your pup at your side, at all times, this can be the ideal dog for you. If you plan on being away from home frequently and cannot take your pup with you, you might just come home someday to a house that has been totally demolished.

On the other hand, if you want a dog that can make you feel safe, a bigger breed may be better for you, but make sure you are not buying a dog that will drag you around the block every time the two of you go for a walk. Similarly, don't by a hunting dog if you expect it to stay in an unfenced yard every time a rabbit hops through or a bird flies by.

Know what you want in a companion and then make some calls and ask about the personalities of the dogs and puppies available. If the breeder does not want to spend the time it takes to answer your questions or bother about what you are looking for, go elsewhere.

Your Dog is Not a Wolf

Your dog is not a wolf, and, as a matter of fact, neither are wolves! Wolves are not the mythical creatures that we read about in fictional books or watch in movies. Wolves live in a very highly evolved society. If the Alpha Wolf always had to fight to stay on top, he would never get everything done that is expected of him.

In wolf society, there are two main wolves, the alpha male and the alpha female, these are the breeding pair. They mate for life. If they live in an area where there are very few wolves around, but game is plentiful, another female and male may also breed and produce puppies.

The alpha wolves move off by themselves, find a place to den, and have their puppies while everyone else is off doing their own thing. When the puppies get to be about six weeks old, the rest of the wolves join back with the alpha pair and everyone helps with the care and training of the newest members of the pack.

This is all voluntary and if someone wants to leave for a while or try a new territory, that wolf is free to go and also welcome to return whenever it wants. The wolves are each where they want to be in the pack and if they want to try something different it is fine with all concerned.

The alpha wolf must be strong enough and a good enough hunter to provide enough food for the whole family until mama wolf can leave the den long enough to hunt. Once the pups are old enough for the mother to leave long enough to do some hunting, the other wolves in the pack babysit whenever she is gone. If the alpha wolf was always fighting to prove he was tough enough to remain the alpha, he would not have the strength to provide for his family when they need him most.

The point of all of this is that you do not need to devote every moment of your relationship with your dog to making sure it recognizes you as the alpha dog in the pack. Most dogs have a sense of humor, and if they get one over on their owner, it is just a fun joke that everyone enjoys.

You can make a mistake and it is not going to alter the relationship with your dog, providing the mistake does not cause the dog serious pain or is repeated frequently. Dogs really are man's best friend, with an emphasis on "friend."

This does not mean that you do not have to set firm limits and on occasion reaffirm those limits. It does mean that you and your dog can be partners and that is what makes owning a dog fun and rewarding.

Working dogs and sporting dogs frequently have to perform their duties while off-leash. If the dog did not want to do those things it could certainly not do them when the owner releases it and gives it the command to perform.

We do not have control over the dog at all times and that is OK, because our dog wants to work with us and enjoys making us happy. Loving your dog is not spoiling it and loving it does not mean it is not going to obey you; just the opposite is true.

Most of the time, our dogs obey us because they want to. We, in turn, should make obeying us easy and pleasant for our dogs.

Key Takeaways:
- You do not need to devote every moment of your relationship with your dog;
- You and your dog can be partners and that is what makes owning a dog fun and rewarding;
- We do not have control over the dog at all times and that is OK, because our dog wants to work with us and enjoys making us happy.

Make Your Home "Pet Friendly"

I had a new owner call me one night, at his wits end. The puppy he had recently purchased was standing at the top of the living room stairs and barking at him like there was going to be no tomorrow and he had no idea what had happened to make his puppy so upset with him.

I started to ask some basic questions about their relationship and quickly realized that his puppy simply had too many rules to learn and follow and that is what she was yelling at him about. There were too many places where she could not go, too many things she could not touch and too many behaviors that had become unacceptable.

She was simply confused and feeling overwhelmed with the all of the "no's" in her life. He had failed to make a "pet friendly" area in his house for her. Once he fixed up the den, where she spent most of her time, so that she could be comfortable in there without a million rules governing her behavior, they became buddies again. He had just not been able to look at his world through her eyes and see that there were too many rules for one little puppy to learn.

Think Like a Dog.

Thinking like a dog sounds easy, but we tend to see the world through our people eyes instead of dog eyes and that can make it difficult to understand what your dog is experimenting. Dogs are pretty straight forward and it is simply up to us to figure out what they are trying to tell us.

If your dog is doing the same behavior over and over again, stop to figure out what it is telling you by doing it. Some behaviors are bred into some dogs and other behaviors are a way of communicating with you.

If you open the door and your pup is out the door, down the walk and halfway to your neighbor's house before you have a chance to pick up the leash, your dog's urge to run and hunt may be a very strong one and you will need to spend time changing some behaviors, but also making sure those behaviors do not keep happening by preventing them.

A fenced in yard or a cable to run on may be easier than the constant battle to keep your dog from running every time it has the chance. Teaching it to sit and wait for you to be ready to go is another way to get your dog to not run whenever you open the door (we will address that behavior, shortly).

If your dog loves to chew things or carry something in its mouth all the time, having plenty of great toys on hand and some that even have goodies in them, is a better choice than always hollering "no!" If your dog is bored most of the time, its behaviors are also going to reflect that.

All dogs need attention and exercise and the younger the dog, the more it needs. When your Irish setter is 12 years old, it may be content to lay by the fireplace all evening and look beautiful, but right now, it needs to be exercised and played with to keep it from getting into trouble.

If you are going to be away from home most of the day, perhaps a playmate is in order for your dog. Dogs crave companionship and another dog can be the answer to preventing separation anxiety, which translates into problem behaviors, every time you leave the house. Learning to think like your dog can help you to solve many of the everyday problems that naturally occur when you own a dog.

Two Methods of Training Your Dog

Most training systems fall under one of two methods: the aversive-based method and the reward-based method. There are some variations of these, but is all comes down to training your dog by using force and punishment or training your dog by using rewards and praise.

Traditional Method (Aversive-Based)

The basic notion of expecting your dog to perform or not perform a specific behavior, and punishing the dog if it does not perform correctly, is based on the traditional or aversive-based method of training.

Punishing a dog for barking, punishing the dog for peeing in the house, punishing the dog for jumping on a stranger to say hello, applying pressure or pain and releasing it when the dog does the correct behavior, tugging on a choke collar until the dog stops pulling and begins to heal and pinching the dog's ear until it opens its mouth to drop a retrieved object are all examples of aversion-based methods of training. They all rely on using punishment if the dog fails to perform as expected.

Reward-Based Method

Showing the dog what you want it to do and rewarding it for doing the correct behavior, waiting for the dog to perform the correct behavior on its own and rewarding it when it spontaneously performs the behavior and having your dog perform a desired behavior instead of an undesired behavior, are all examples of reward-based methods.

You can certainly see why the dog would prefer that you use reward-based training methods! Unfortunately, each method has its strong points and its week points. Even trying to use a combination of the two methods has strong and weak points.

Traditional methods of dog training can produce results pretty quickly, and that is the biggest draw they have. These methods can also result in a dog that is afraid of you or refuses to do anything for you because it does not know when it will or will not get punished or one that learns that you will not really punish it hard enough to make a difference, so why not ignore you all together?

Reward-based methods require some planning and sometimes some tricky thinking and the results may take longer to achieve. The bright side, though, is your dog will love all the treats it gets and will not become afraid of you. It will also not do forbidden behaviors behind your back when it thinks it can get away with it.

I was a traditional trainer for about 20 years and when I decided to look into reward-based training methods, it really did take a little while for it all to make sense to me.

One of the reasons I started looking into an alternative method of training was because people were bring me dogs that had been "ruined" by harsh methods of training and wanted me to "fix" them. To do this, I had to do some research and find alternative methods that could undo someone else's mistakes. That was when I stumbled across the reward-based methods and realized I had discovered something very special.

There are two basic ideas in reward-based training, reward the dog for doing the right behavior and reward the dog for doing something different than the wrong behavior.

The first is pretty easy and straight forward. The second takes a bit more work, but the reward for the dog owner is a lot of satisfaction.

Rewarding Your Dog for the Right Behavior

Remember this sage advice: Do not allow your puppy or little dog to do anything you would not allow a 60 pound full grown dog to do. Teaching your pup to do the correct behaviors at 2 pounds is so much easier that teaching it at 60 pounds. Also, a yappy 5 pond adult dog is just as annoying as a 60 pound barker.

First, always have small, easy and quick to eat, very desirable treats on hand. This is the biggest secret to starting reward-based training. Once your dog learns the correct behaviors, substitute praise for treats, but always plan on keeping an occasional favorite treat on hand for a reward for performing desirable behaviors. Your pup will love you for it.

The three commands that can change your (and your dog's) life are:

"Sit," "Down" and "Close Mouth"

The basic idea of reward-based training is that you break down every behavior you want your dog to perform, into small steps. That way you can reward it every time it learns one of the steps and then move on to the next step.

When you are training your dog or puppy, the best rule is to only make the training session last about five to ten minutes, tops. Also, always try to end the training session on a positive note so you can give your pup one last treat and then signal that the session is over.

Make training fun and enjoyable and it will become a source of quality time spent together instead of a grueling nightmare that you both resent.

If you are teaching your dog to sit, you show the dog what you want it to do by placing it in a sitting position and saying "sit" and giving it a treat when it sits. If you want the dog to stay there, you can use the command, "stay." Hold your finger up and count to three and give it another treat to reward the dog for staying. If your dog or puppy does not sit for the required count, sit it back down and repeat the process.

Remember: dogs learn differently than people do. If you get angry or short of patience, break down the steps into even smaller or shorter increments; this helps the dog to be successful each time and allows it to learn one step at a time. If you do this often enough, your dog will learn to sit on command.

Sounds pretty basic, doesn't it? Now, once you have taught it to sit. With the treat in your hand, let the dog sniff the treat while you lower the hand closer and closer to the floor, giving the dog the command "down" and give the dog the treat when it lies all the way down on the floor. Remind the dog to "stay," and give it another treat for staying there.

You just taught your dog two commands; "sit/stay" and "down" using a reward-based training method. These are two very important commands so they are always the best two to start with. We will come back to these two again, and again.

"Close mouth" is also an important command to each your dog. This one can be a little tricky because it is difficult to train a dog to close its mouth when its mouth is not open. You may have to wait for the right opportunity to train this behavior.

Start by using the "sit" command and get your dog sitting in front of you. If its mouth is open, give it the command, "close mouth," gently close its mouth, hold it shut for the count of three, and then reward it with a treat.

Just like you held a finger up to signal how long your pup should stay in the sit position, hold your finger where it can see it and know how long it has to keep its mouth closed. This is actually a difficult behavior for your dog to do and understand, so go slowly with this one.

Practice "sit/stay," "down" and "close mouth" on a regular basis. Do not always reward the behavior with a treat; use praise at times and treats at times and this will keep the behavior happening on command for the life of your dog. When you are training your dog to respond to commands, remember the rule about keeping training sessions short and do not expect your dog to hold these positions for a long period of time when first learning them, especially if you are working with a very young dog.

The Terrible Twos

Did I tell you that puppies have a tendency to go through the "terrible twos?" There will come a period of time, somewhere between a year and a half and two years where your dog is going to suddenly "unlearn" everything you have taught it.

Be patient and remember to maintain your rules and boundaries and one day, without warning, the "terrible twos" will be over with and your loving companion will be back and more mature than ever before.

As a dog trainer, I have seen this happen over and over again and I have spent long hours on the phone assuring owners that their dog really was going to work its way out of this stage and be a great dog again.

I believe it is just our puppies' way of going through their adolescence and they seem to go through it like a typical teenager; testing limits and pretending they have forgotten all the rules for about a period of four to six months. At least it does not last as long as human teen rebellion generally does.

House-Breaking

If you have a brand new puppy, no matter how small, have a place, near where it spends most of its time for potty-training. Newspapers or commercial pads both work fine. Initially, it is all in the timing.

Set the pup on the paper or pad several times an hour, and tell it to "go potty" or whatever command you would like to use. When the puppy does relieve itself there, praise it and give it lots of love. If the puppy goes somewhere else, do not punish it, just set it on the paper and remind it that that is the place to use.

When the pup uses the pad correctly, praise and even giving it a treat will get you some quick results. Remember to keep the paper close by so the puppy has quick access to it. Puppies do not have full control of their functions until they are about six months old, so plan on lots of reminders and treats for doing it correctly.

If you plan on having you pup eventually go outside to relieve itself, you can gradually start moving the potty pad closer to the door.

The other method that you can combine with this is to pick up your puppy frequently and take it outside and give it the command to relieve itself. Just remember that early training relies on timing, and lots of praise for doing it right will go a long ways.

If you need to house break an adult dog, possibly because it has never lived in a house before, the procedure is pretty much the same.

Take it outside, on a leash several times a day and particularly upon waking and immediately after a meal, an hour after a meal and just before bed. Always praise a puppy or dog for relieving itself where it is supposed to. A small treat for rewarding the right behavior is always a happy reward to get when you are a dog.

Some dogs hate to relieve themselves when on a leash. The best "fix" for this issue is to spend a day in the country and walk your dog and keep it on the leash until it finally gives in and relieves itself. That is the time for tremendous praise and a special treat.

So far, I have never heard of a dog needing to do the all day outing more than twice to get the idea that you want it to go potty when on the leash and it will not get into trouble for doing so.

Telling You When it is Time to go Outside

Do you want your dog to ring a bell to tell you it wants out? This is fun and a great idea if you might get too busy and forget to automatically take your dog outside. You can buy special bells made for this purpose or you can even buy very inexpensive Christmas bells that are made to hang over the doorknob that work as well.

When it is time to take your puppy or dog outside, walk it over to the door and nudge the bell with your hand to make it ring before going outside. Do this several times and then stand there quietly by the door the next time it is time to go out and wait to see if the dog will decide to nudge the bell for you (Some dogs pick up on this one quickly).

If the dog does not do anything but wait at the door, jingle the bell and proceed outside as usual. The next time it is time to go outside, stand by the door a little longer to see if the dog will nudge the bell. If the dog does anything that does make the bell ring, praise the dog and proceed outside. Repeat this every time you take it outside.

Before long, your dog will be going to the door to ring the bell when it needs to go outside. All it takes is a little patience.

Obedience and Incompatible behaviors

Sometimes there are behaviors that you do not want your dog to do, such as jump on someone to say hello. It is easier to train the dog to do a behavior that is more desirable than to not do any behavior.

Confused yet? Here is the best example: if your dog loves to jump on people to say hello, it cannot jump and sit at the same time, so command your dog to sit instead of jump and then have the person come over and say hello to your canine buddy.

If your dog gets too excited around new people to maintain a sitting position, have it go all the way "down;" this is a little easier to maintain for your dog. Make sure the person who was the reason for the excitement pets your dog so it knows it will get what it wanted but needs to use a different behavior to get it.

Knowing a basic command like "sit" or "down" can work remarkably well to avoid problem behaviors. Your dog cannot run, jump, chase or do many other behaviors if it is sitting or lying down. When in doubt, have your dog sit or lie down while you work out what you want it to do or not to do.

To repeat what I was telling you earlier: Make sure that you and your dog practice these commands frequently, and even teach your dog to respond to this command from a distance.

Teach it to sit, on command, from a distance and then stay there until you approach and release it. Use signals and praise and treats and reinforce this one command frequently. You do not need to give your dog a treat every time it does the behavior correctly, but on occasion, give it a favorite treat and lots of praise and love for performing the behavior.

This can not only prevent some problem behaviors from occurring, it can possibly save your dog's life if it is heading in a direction where it may be in danger.

Barking

Barking can be one of the most problematic behaviors to deal with because of two reasons: First, there are several reasons why dogs bark, so we do not always know what has triggered the behavior, and Second, it is also something that frequently happens when no one is around to deal with the behavior and this causes problems for your neighbors.

You hear the dog barking and it may sound the same to you each time, but your dog may be attempting to tell you something different each time it barks. A bark may mean, "There is a stranger lurking too near the door," or "my water dish is empty and I am really thirsty," or "I am bored to death so I think I will bark and try to get some attention," to ultimately, "my owners are gone and I am afraid they will never come home again." All we, as humans hear, though, is "bark, bark, bark."

Barking is communication and it is important to know why your dog is barking. If it is telling you that there is danger close by, you certainly do not want to ignore that bark, you want to investigate the reason. The same if your dog is telling you that something is wrong like the water dish is empty or it has to go outside before it pees on the floor.

Sadly, some dogs just plain become nuisance barkers and these dogs frequently end up at shelters. Many small breeds are known for this trait and their owners end up abandoning their pets other than trying to work out the best way to deal with the problem.

There are really only a couple of problems that cannot be worked out with a little thought and effort, and, with the electronic aides now available on the market, barking is no longer one of those reasons.

We have talked about using incompatible behaviors, and one behavior that is incompatible with barking is to have a closed mouth. Approach your dog, have it sit and then tell it to "close mouth." If the dog continues to try to bark or barks as soon as you release it from the command (remember, do not attempt to have the dog maintain this behavior for very long), you will need to further investigate why it is barking.

It is important to understand what your dog is telling you when it barks. Every bark should be investigated. Remember, your dog really is trying to tell you something. Finding the reason for the bark and correcting it is often all that is needed.

If your dog is barking because you are not available to do what it wants, you may not be available to stop it from barking or you may be too busy to give it the time your dog is demanding.

I have some very close friends who have a dog that loves to bark whenever there is company visiting, if the company is allergic to dogs so this dog cannot come out and stay with everyone. She will bark like crazy and be very annoying, just like a little kid. She is being forced to stay in her bedroom when she would rather be visiting the company and she lets us all know how she feels about it.

There are now devices available to stop nuisance barking that work well and are not expensive. There are bark collars that emit a sound that can make your dog stop barking, there are collars that can spray water that stops the bark and collars that will give the dog a slight shock when it barks.

I always ask people to consult their veterinarian for a suggestion because your local vet can generally be relied upon more than some commercial website that only wants your money. My friend with the barking dog uses an electric bark collar that first emits a high pitched noise then delivers a low-level stimulus. After the first time she wore the collar, she does not bark at all when she is wearing it.

Remember, bark collars are a last resort, but are much better than abandoning your dog because it is a nuisance barker. Most dogs can be quickly taught to not bark in one or two sessions with a bark collar. These collars have made a huge difference in the reasons people bring dogs to shelters, with excessive barking no longer taking the number one position.

Healing or Walking with a Slack Leash

There are several devises on the market designed to prevent dogs from pulling when they are being walked. The device called a "head collar" seems to work the best and stops the dog from pulling, humanely-for both dog and master.

You can use these devices forever or use them as a training aid; it is up to you and your dog. If you do not know which one to get, ask your vet, he or she will generally have a preference. These training aids are not that expensive, and the small investment is well worth it. Again, have treats ready and start out with some basic commands.

If you have a small puppy, it is much easier to start the basics at a very young age. If you have an older dog, the basics still work; it just takes a little longer. Just remember the key phrase: do not let your puppy or small dog do anything you would not allow a large dog to do.

What does your dog or puppy do when you put on your coat or reach for the leash? Does it go ballistic? Once you have the leash on and head for the door, does it drag you out outside at the speed of light? If you live where there is sometimes snow or ice, this behavior can actually be dangerous.

Do not put up with this. It is actually very easy to change this behavior; it just takes a bit of planning and some patience. This is another time when incompatible behaviors come into play.

Again, remember your two commands, "sit" and "down." When it is time to put on the leash, make your pup sit while you attach the leash to its collar. When it actually is time to open the door, if the puppy is tugging at the leash, again make it stop and sit. If you have a non-pull device on your dog, this will help.

You do not want your dog to pull you out the door; if you have any steps to deal with, you could fall or trip, and one of you could get hurt. Remember, anytime your dog is doing a behavior that you do not desire, have it sit until it settles down and is willing to pay attention to you.

The first time or two you do this, give yourself plenty of time and stop and sit whenever you need to. The key is having the time to do it right.

If you choose to do this when you are running late for work, it just might not go very well. If you do this on a Saturday morning when you have plenty of time, it will be a rewarding experience for both of you.

As your dog soon learns to walk with a slack leash, you can move to a more conventional leash and leave to training leash at home.

www.ingramcontent.com/pod-product-compliance
Lightning Source LLC
Chambersburg PA
CBHW022011170726
47994CB00023B/3099